the Holy Spirit

Scott Petty

Little Black Books: The Holy Spirit
© Matthias Media 2012

Matthias Media
(St Matthias Press Ltd ACN 067 558 365)
PO Box 225
Kingsford NSW 2032
Australia
Telephone: (02) 9663 1478; international: +61-2-9663-1478
Facsimile: (02) 9663 3265; international: +61-2-9663-3265
Email: info@matthiasmedia.com.au
Internet: www.matthiasmedia.com.au

Matthias Media (USA)
Telephone: 330 953 1702; international: +1-330-953-1702
Facsimile: 330 953 1712; international: +1-330-953-1712
Email: sales@matthiasmedia.com
Internet: www.matthiasmedia.com

Scripture taken from the Holy Bible, NEW INTERNATIONAL VERSION®. Copyright © 1973, 1978, 1984 by Biblica, Inc. All rights reserved worldwide. Used by permission.

ISBN 978 1 921896 42 2

Cover design and typesetting by Matthias Media.

Contents

CHAPTER 1

Meet the Holy Spirit

Do you believe in ghosts? I don't—not just because I've never seen one, but also because I find it very difficult to believe the people who claim to have seen one. On the internet, people who have spotted ghosts can share their stories and photos with other believers right across the world. One day when I happened upon a ghost story website, I kept reading because I was interested to see if I could be convinced. There were a whole bunch of stories called things like 'The Lone Wolf' and 'The Banshee's Curse' and 'Walter in the Basement' and other odd names, and the tales they told seemed pretty silly to me.

I kept looking, though, because I was intrigued to see what the photos page would reveal, with all its 'clear examples' of paranormal activity. There was one photo entitled 'Freddy Jackson', where behind the top row in a group photo you could see the shadowy face of another man. There was another photo called 'The Ghost of Boothill Cemetery'. Some dude in America was taking photos of his friend, who was dressed up in old Western gear, standing among the gravestones. Which is ok I guess if you're into that sort of thing. Anyway, in the background of the photo, just to the right of his costumed friend, is an image of what appears to be a thin man in a dark hat. This apparently convinced the photographer that ghosts were real. But as I looked at these photos, I realized I'd seen this sort of thing in other places. I'd seen it in magazines, where people 'photo bomb' celebrity photos, popping into the paparazzo's photo at just the right time.

Given the reality of photo-bombers and of photo-editing software, websites like this are never going to convince me that ghosts are real. I remain sceptical about the existence of ghosts.

And yet the Scriptures teach me to believe in the Holy Spirit, who is also sometimes referred to as the Holy Ghost. What are you and I supposed to think about the Holy Spirit if we find it so difficult to believe in ghosts? We understand God the Father because we get what fathers are supposed to be like, even if our own fathers aren't great. We can visualize Jesus, God the Son, because he became a man and walked among us. But what about

God the Holy Spirit? It's pretty confusing. And it's even more confusing because in some churches you barely hear any mention of the Holy Spirit, while in others the Holy Spirit seems to be all you hear about.

So I think it would do us all good to examine the Holy Spirit from the words of the Bible, which the Holy Spirit co-wrote as he spoke through the human authors like the prophets and apostles (2 Pet 1:20-21). My hope is that by the end of this Little Black Book you won't just be a believer in the Holy Spirit, but you will also understand who he is, what he does, and how fortunate and blessed we are to have him.

Well then, the first thing we need to do is meet the Holy Spirit.

The Holy Spirit is God

If we are to truly meet the Holy Spirit we need to know that he is God. He is part of that unique thing in Christianity called the Trinity, in which there are three persons—Father, Son and Holy Spirit—within the one being of God. Let me say straight up that if you don't understand how there can be three persons who are each fully God and yet together are just one God, join the club. Nobody understands it properly and nobody can explain it with absolute clarity. I reckon that's a clue that it's not made up—because who would make up a story with three persons who form just one God? But even if we cannot fully understand the Trinity, it's impossible not to notice the idea in the Bible. God the Father is God, God the Son (Jesus) is God, and God the Holy Spirit is also God. They are all equally and fully God, but there are not three Gods, just the one. You notice this in what Jesus said to his disciples at the very end of Matthew's Gospel:

> "Therefore go and make disciples of all nations, baptizing them in the name of the Father and of the Son and of the Holy Spirit, and teaching them to obey everything I have commanded you…" (Matt 28:19-20)

So according to Jesus there is only one name—he doesn't tell his disciples to baptize new disciples into three names. There is one name because there's one God. But there are three persons: Father, Son and Spirit. This can become confusing as you try to get your head around it. You may have heard analogies or illustrations that try to help explain it. Like if you think of God as if he were an egg, there is only one egg but the yellow yolk, the egg white and the shell are three different parts of that one egg. The problem with this illustration is that you'd never describe the eggshell as the complete egg, or the yolk or the white alone as 'fully the egg'. But the Scriptures teach us that God the Father, Jesus, and the Holy Spirit are each fully God. So the egg illustration is only useful up to a point.

Or you might have heard people say that God is like water. With water there is only one substance: H_2O. But H_2O can appear distinctly as ice, or liquid water, or steam. It's all water, but there are distinctive features depending on whether it's solid, liquid or gas. Again, this sort of helps, but not completely, because you can never find water, ice and steam in the same place under the same conditions. And yet you do find God the Father, Jesus and the Holy Spirit in the same place at the same time. This happens, for example, at the baptism of Jesus, which we read about in Matthew 3:

> As soon as Jesus was baptized, he went up out of the water. At that moment heaven was opened, and he saw the Spirit of God descending like a dove and lighting on him. And a voice from heaven said, "This is my Son, whom I love; with him I am well pleased". (Matt 3:16-17)

Here you have in one place God the Son being baptized, God the

Holy Spirit descending upon Jesus, and God the Father speaking from heaven. Each one is fully God at the same time. So again, the water illustration is helpful up to a point, but not completely accurate.

At the end of the day, no human illustration is going to be absolutely clear because God is beyond the human mind. And although it is worth thinking through how God can be three persons yet just one God, it's not worth getting too hung up about it. It shows us that God is far more complex than our weenie little brains can comprehend.

But for now, it really is worth noting that without doubt the Holy Spirit is God. In fact, he always has been God. If you turn to the very first lines of the Bible you see the Holy Spirit involved in the creation of the world. Take a look at Genesis 1:

> In the beginning God created the heavens and the earth. Now the earth was formless and empty, darkness was over the surface of the deep, and the Spirit of God was hovering over the waters. (Gen 1:1-2)

At creation—way back in the beginning—the Holy Spirit was there, hovering over the watery chaos like a rescue helicopter, ready to put the commands of God into action. The Holy Spirit is God;

he always has been, and he was active from the very beginning.

Not only that, but the Holy Spirit is also a person and he's personal. Just as God the Father is personal, so the Holy Spirit is personal. He's not some strange impersonal power like 'the Force' in the *Star Wars* movies. I'm not saying he has a body like a person— he is called the Holy *Spirit*, after all. But he has personal qualities like intelligence and emotions. The New Testament tells us he can be resisted, grieved or saddened, and he can be lied to. He also does personal things like teach, comfort and guide us. It is interesting to see how Jesus describes the Holy Spirit to the disciples:

> "And I will ask the Father, and he will give you another Counsellor
> to be with you forever—the Spirit of truth. The world cannot accept
> him, because it neither sees him nor knows him. But you know him,
> for he lives with you and will be in you." (John 14:16-17)

Notice that Jesus calls the Holy Spirit a "Counsellor", which is a personal kind of word. And he keeps calling the Holy Spirit "him", not "it", even though you would normally say "it" in the Greek language that the New Testament is written in. Jesus is making the point that the Holy Spirit is a person, not an impersonal force. The Holy Spirit is a "he", not an "it".

The Holy Spirit in the Old Testament

So that shows us who the Holy Spirit is from eternity past. We've seen that he has always been God and that he was involved in the creation of the world. The next question is whether he was active and involved in Old Testament times after creation. As it turns out, he was. But here's the thing: he wasn't given to everyone. God gave the Holy Spirit only to a very few special people.

My friend Katie is a preschool teacher, and she tells me that it's not unusual for preschool kids to think their teachers actually live at the school. Since it's the only place the kids ever see their teachers, they just assume it's where the teachers live. They imagine that when all the kids go home, the teachers get out the dinosaurs and start playing with them, or get into some after-hours finger-painting action. But there is more to life than preschool for the preschool teachers. Once they leave the schoolyard, they aren't in that role of teacher any more. They might be a mother, or a sister, or a softball player.

It seems that in the Old Testament, the Holy Spirit was really only given to particular people, and usually for a particular job or task. This would sort of be like him being given to a teacher for the task of teaching, but not for her tasks as a mother or softball player. The Holy Spirit wasn't usually given to people for their whole lives and for every aspect of their lives, but only to particular people for a particular purpose.

He was sometimes given to the leaders of Israel, like the judges and the early kings, to equip them for the task of leading the people. The judges of Israel, who were more like military leaders than courtroom officials with silly wigs, are a classic example. In Judges 3 we read about Othniel, and how "The Spirit of the LORD came upon him, so that he became Israel's judge and went to war" (v. 10). As for Samson, everyone's favourite hairy hero, Judges 14 tells us that "The Spirit of the LORD came upon him in power so that he tore the lion apart with his bare hands as he might have torn a young goat" (v. 6). Or there's the case of King David. When David was chosen to replace Saul as king over Israel, "Samuel took the horn of oil and anointed him... and from that day on the Spirit of the LORD came upon David in power" (1 Sam 16:13). God gave his Spirit to his anointed and chosen king to equip him for leadership of the people.

God also gave the Holy Spirit to the prophets to equip them for the task of bringing God's message to the people. So the prophet Ezekiel is recorded in Ezekiel 2:2-3 as saying, "As he [the LORD] spoke, the Spirit came into me and raised me to my feet, and I heard him speaking to me. He said: 'Son of man, I am sending you to the Israelites, to a rebellious nation…'" The Holy Spirit was given to the prophets to empower them as they went to give a difficult and unpopular message to rebellious people. Even a craftsman called Bezalel was filled with the Holy Spirit, it says in Exodus 31, to build and furnish the tabernacle—the ornate tent where the people worshipped God as they wandered around in the desert. That sort of assistance would definitely help you to ace woodwork at school, or impress the boss at the building site.

But in the Old Testament the Holy Spirit was only given to leaders, to prophets and priests, and at a stretch to a craftsman, for the particular tasks for which God had chosen them. And as time wore on in Old Testament days, and as God's appointed leaders disappointed time and again, there was a growing expectation that God would send a Spirit-filled leader who would do a better job than any of the judges and kings who had served Israel in the past. More than anyone else, the prophet Isaiah expressed this hope and expectation. He looked forward to a Spirit-filled king in David's line who would prosper where David failed (Isa 11:1-9), a Spirit-filled servant who would bring gentle justice to the nations (Isa

42:1-4), and a Spirit-filled preacher who would bring a message of good news to the poor and downhearted (Isa 61:1-3).

As you ponder who could possibly fulfil such lofty expectations, let's return to the basic fact that in Old Testament days the Holy Spirit wasn't given to ordinary folk—to mum and dad and the kids, or people like you and me. And when you read the later prophets you get the vibe that people longed for the day when there was not just another Spirit-filled leader as Isaiah so hoped, but when all the people of God would be given the Holy Spirit. Ezekiel spoke this message of God to a beaten-up, downtrodden and depressed group of his people:

> "I will give you a new heart and put a new spirit in you; I will
> remove from you your heart of stone and give you a heart of
> flesh. And I will put my Spirit in you and move you to follow my
> decrees." (Ezek 36:26-27)

Something more than just a great leader was needed. People needed God's own Spirit within them. They needed God's Spirit to move their spirits to long to want to go God's way rather than wandering off without him. They needed God's Spirit not just for the leader but for all the people. That's the hope and expectation in Ezekiel

36. Again, in Joel 2:28-32 the prophet Joel told the people that a day would come when God would pour out his Spirit on all his people. Sons and daughters, old men and young men, even servants would all be given the Holy Spirit and would speak of God's truth.

The Holy Spirit and us

And that's why, if you are a Christian, it is truly awesome to know that the day Joel described has come. After Jesus left the earth, God poured the Holy Spirit into every Christian heart.

About the same time I was scooting around the internet looking at ghost stories, I came across another photo that was tricky to accurately identify. It looked like a dish of spaghetti or perhaps those bean sprouts you sometimes find in Asian salads. But it was in fact a dish full of intestinal worms. They were parasitic worms that live inside the stomach and intestines of animals and humans. They weren't tiny either; they were about the size of noodles or bean sprouts (which means I will never look at spaghetti in the same way again). And as I was reading the accompanying article, I learned—and I guess this must be true because it was on the internet—that approximately one in three Americans have parasitic worms living in their stomach and intestines.

Obviously, worms aren't good for you. But a whole bunch of people are carrying worms around inside of them, and yet they don't feel any different. The Scriptures tell us that one in every one Christian person has the Holy Spirit living in them (e.g. Rom 8:9), yet many of us don't feel any different. Partly that's because he doesn't physically live within us like a worm does. He is spirit, so he lives within our spirits. But regardless of whether you feel any different, if you are a Christian then you have the blessing of the Holy Spirit in you. You have the Spirit in the way that God's people of old could only dream of and long for. Remember the words of Jesus:

> "I will ask the Father, and he will give you another Counsellor to be with you forever—the Spirit of truth. The world cannot accept him, because it neither sees him nor knows him. But you know him, for he lives with you and will be in you." (John 14:16-17)

What Jesus said to those first disciples is true for every disciple or follower of Jesus since then. We know the Holy Spirit and he is in us. You cannot know God without the Holy Spirit, but if you know God and you follow Jesus then I can guarantee you that the

Holy Spirit lives within you. The Spirit has taken up residence in your spirit. He has made his home in your soul. God is always with you because the Spirit is in you. You may not feel any different. That's because it's a spiritual thing, not a physical thing. And the Holy Spirit may not draw attention to himself there (but that's because his job is to draw attention to Jesus, which is what we'll take a look at in the next chapter).

But it's important to understand that if you are a Christian, if you follow Jesus, it is the Holy Spirit in you who has made God real to you. He is not given to just a few special people any more; he is given to every Christian, now that Jesus has left the world. He wasn't just active and involved in creation; he's active and involved in your life. The Holy Spirit who was promised in the Old Testament has been poured out into your life. So God is always with you. He can never leave you.

If you're not a Christian you might be thinking, "This is pretty weird. I'm not all that sure that I want any spirit living inside me. I think I'd rather have intestinal worms—at least I know I can get them out if I go to the hospital. I'm ok with the God stuff—even the Jesus bit is all right—but you have lost me with that Holy Spirit stuff." If this describes you, then here's what you need to understand: you cannot know God and you cannot follow Jesus without having the Holy Spirit. He is also known as the Spirit of God and the Spirit of Christ. You cannot get the Holy Spirit without being a Christian, but you also cannot be a Christian without getting the Holy Spirit. Romans 8:9 tells us that "if anyone does not have the Spirit of Christ, he does not belong to Christ". So if you're thinking, "What would I want with the Holy Spirit?" the answer is God; the answer is Jesus. You want the Holy Spirit because he is the way that God becomes real to us; he is the way we see our need for God; and he is the way by which we can follow Jesus. And he's not just for the hero Christians. He is for every single person who calls on the name of Jesus. So he is someone you ought to want in your life, because our need for God is very real.

You may have started this chapter being an unbeliever when it comes to ghosts. And you may never have thought much about the Holy Spirit. Hopefully you are now convinced that he is real, that he is God, that he always has been, and that he now lives in all Christians. Jesus had to leave, but God by his Spirit is always with us and will never leave.

CHAPTER 2

The Holy Spirit and Jesus

As a fan of old-school stripped-back sweaty electric rock 'n' roll,
I've been to a few stadium rock concerts in my time. After the
opening blast of wall-to-wall sound that knocks the earth off its
orbit, there is usually this part of the concert where the bass player
and the drummer—the 'muscle' of the band—go off stage for a
drink. And perhaps the guitarist swaps his Fender Stratocaster
(that's an electric guitar, for those of you who only listen to boy
bands and pop princesses) for an acoustic guitar. Or maybe the
lead singer sits down at a piano. And the stadium goes dark except
for a lone spotlight that casts its brilliant glare on the guitarist or
pianist. The whole little caper is supposed to highlight what an
amazing musician the dude is, but visually it's a pretty basic set-up.
There's just one man on stage playing an instrument with a bright
spotlight shining its luminous beam upon him. And that's it really.

Just the dude under the glare of the light.

If you can sketch that picture in your mind—of the musician in the spotlight—then you have yourself a really good illustration of how Jesus and the Holy Spirit fit together in the Christian faith. At the end of the day, *Christ*ianity is about Christ. Jesus is the focus of attention; he is in the limelight, and our gaze is upon him. And the Holy Spirit is like the spotlight. The Holy Spirit exists to shine light onto Jesus rather than bring attention to himself. You wouldn't necessarily pick this up from some Christians who make it sound like the Holy Spirit is the focus of attention today. But to think that Jesus has somehow faded into the shadows and that the Holy Spirit is on centre stage would be like watching the lone musician under the light and talking about how great the spotlight is, how well it was designed, or how brilliantly it shone. That would be a strange thing to talk about when the purpose of the spotlight is to draw attention to the man playing the music rather than to draw attention to itself.

We have just seen how the Holy Spirit was busy in the Old Testament, both in the creation of the world and in equipping the leaders and prophets of Israel in their jobs as judges, kings and prophets. But we also saw that something better was required—

not just a new Spirit-filled leader but also the gift of the Holy Spirit for all of God's people, from the greatest to the least. So it ought to be a great encouragement to us as Christians that we live in the day when the Holy Spirit *has* been poured out into the lives of every person who loves God and follows Jesus. God will never leave us, because his Spirit is in us.

But before we motor on to explaining the difference that the Holy Spirit makes to our Christian lives, we need to back up a bit and see how Jesus and the Holy Spirit fit together. When we do that, we discover a couple of special things about Jesus and the Holy Spirit.

Jesus was the special man of the Spirit

The first thing we discover is that Jesus was the special—the one and only—man of the Spirit in his own lifetime. Because we are used to the idea that the Holy Spirit is given to all Christians, it doesn't occur to us that it wasn't like that in the time of Jesus. We automatically think that the Holy Spirit operated in Jesus' day in the same way that he operates today. But that's not quite right. In the era of the Gospels, in Jesus' lifetime, he was the one and only man of the Spirit.

I'm sure what I'm about to say is true of many different sports in many different eras, but for the sport of basketball the 1990s were a magical period. Even if basketball is not as popular outside the US now, it was massive during the 1990s. Partly this was because everyone seemed to want to be American. Some people wanted to be gangsta rappers, others wanted to be pro basketballers; some wanted to be both. But the real reason basketball was the number one sport everywhere can be summed up in two words: Michael Jordan.

Back in the 90s, if I asked you who the best basketballer in the world was, there was only one name: Jordan. Michael Jordan: Chicago Bulls captain and undisputed all-round legend. Jordan took the Chicago Bulls to the championships three years in a row, not once but twice in the 90s. He won five MVP awards and six NBA Finals MVP awards, was selected for the All-NBA First Team ten times, and attained many other awards. He still holds the NBA records for highest career regular season scoring average and highest career playoff scoring average. In 1999, he was named the greatest North American athlete of the 20th century by the sports network ESPN. He is the reason why Nike is the top sports brand in the world. He was the unique man of basketball in the 1990s.

Just like Jordan, Jesus was the unique man of the Spirit in the era of the Gospels. If you thought 'Holy Spirit', you thought 'Jesus'. He was the main man when it came to the Holy Spirit.

You see this in the Gospels of Matthew, Mark and Luke. Firstly, you see it in what they don't say about the Holy Spirit. In Mark's Gospel there are virtually no references to the Holy Spirit as he relates to other believers. In Matthew and Luke there are only a couple more. This is amazing when you think about it because Matthew, Mark and Luke lived in the time covered by the book of Acts—in fact, Luke wrote the book of Acts. And the book of Acts is filled with stories of amazing things that happened when the Holy Spirit was given to Christians. But instead of including all that they later experienced of the Spirit in the Gospel accounts, the Gospel writers stuck to what actually happened in Jesus' life. This not only gives you great confidence about the historical reliability of the Gospel accounts; it also teaches us that Jesus was the special man of the Spirit in his own lifetime.

What Matthew, Mark and Luke do say about the Holy Spirit and Jesus makes it even clearer that the Holy Spirit brings attention to Jesus. Jesus was the one who fulfilled Isaiah's hopes for the new and better Spirit-filled leader and preacher that we looked at in the previous chapter. He was the special man of the Spirit. About the birth of Jesus, Matthew says, "This is how the birth of Jesus Christ came about: His mother Mary was pledged to be married to Joseph, but before they came together, she was found to be with child through the Holy Spirit" (Matt 1:18). About the baptism of Jesus, Matthew says, "As soon as Jesus was baptized, he went up out of the water. At that moment heaven was opened, and he saw the Spirit of God descending like a dove and lighting on him" (Matt 3:16). Just a few verses later Matthew tells us, "Then Jesus was led by the Spirit into the desert to be tempted by the devil" (Matt 4:1). If you think to yourself that this has never happened to you, it's worth remembering that it didn't happen to anyone else either.

At about the same point in Luke's Gospel, Jesus quotes the prophecy from Isaiah 61 about the coming Spirit-filled preacher and applies it to himself with these words: "The Spirit of the Lord is on me, because he has anointed me to preach good news to the poor" (Luke 4:18). And what is true of his teaching is just as true of his miracles, healings and driving out of demons. Jesus is the special man of the Spirit. Even John the Baptist (who was the most out-there spiritual dude of his time and who many people thought was The One—the Messiah) said about Jesus, "I baptize you with water. But one more powerful than I will come… he will baptize you with the Holy Spirit" (Luke 3:16). In his lifetime Jesus was the special man of the Spirit. If you think 'basketball in the 1990s', you think 'Jordan'. If you think 'Holy Spirit in the Gospels', you must think 'Jesus'.

Jesus is the special giver of the Spirit

So that's cool. Jesus was the Holy Spirit guy during his lifetime. But what about after that? Well, what we discover then is that Jesus is the special giver of the Spirit. You see this readily from Jesus' words in John's Gospel. The most concentrated section of teaching we have about the Holy Spirit comes from Jesus in John 14-16. In only a couple of verses, Jesus says:

> "When the Counsellor comes, whom I will send to you from the Father, the Spirit of truth who goes out from the Father, he will testify about me…" (John 15:26)

> "But I tell you the truth: It is for your good that I am going away. Unless I go away, the Counsellor will not come to you; but if I go, I will send him to you." (John 16:7)

In these two verses it is clear that the Holy Spirit, who is sometimes called the Counsellor, is a gift from Jesus. He did not give the Holy Spirit to his followers until after he left the earth, which we'll think about in the next chapter. But what Jesus promised to his followers in John 14—the gift of the Holy Spirit—he delivered to his followers after he went back to heaven.

Like many Australians I have spent a few years living in London, which really is a terrific city. But as an Aussie in London you miss a few things from home—like seeing the sun, wearing shorts, going outdoors, that sort of thing. To be honest it's not really that bad; sometimes they even get a summer. And you can buy things like Vegemite in the supermarkets over there. But the killer is that you cannot get Australia's favourite chocolate biscuits—Tim Tams—in the supermarkets. As far as I know you can only get Tim Tams from one shop in England; it's called the Australia Shop down in the West End of London. So when you get homesick and lonely in London, you have to trundle your sorry butt off to the Australia Shop to get your Tim Tams. It's the only supplier of Tim Tams in England.

That's a little bit like the Holy Spirit and Jesus. When it comes to the Holy Spirit, Jesus is the only supplier. You cannot get the Holy Spirit from anywhere or anyone other than Jesus.

So the question is not who: Jesus. The question is not even when: after he left the world and at the time you become a believer. The question is why: why does Jesus give the Holy Spirit to his followers? And again, if you look in John's Gospel, it seems that Jesus gives the Holy Spirit so that the Spirit can be, for all his followers in every place and every generation, what Jesus was for his disciples in Israel during his lifetime. Jesus gave the Holy Spirit to the original twelve disciples to guide them and teach them and remind them of everything he said while he was here:

> The Counsellor, the Holy Spirit, whom the Father will send in my name, will teach you all things and will remind you of everything I have said to you. (John 14:26)

But that applies not just to the twelve disciples, but also to all disciples since then. What Jesus was for the twelve, the Holy Spirit is for all of Jesus' followers. It works a little like this: as Jesus was God's gift to the world ("For God so loved the world that he gave his one and only Son"; John 3:16), so the Holy Spirit is Jesus' gift to all his followers, wherever and whenever they live ("if I go, I will send him to you"; John 16:7 again).

Just as Jesus represented God to us, so the Holy Spirit represents

Jesus to us. In John 15 Jesus says, "When the Counsellor comes, whom I will send to you from the Father, the Spirit of truth... he will testify about me" (v. 26). The Spirit doesn't represent himself; he represents Jesus. In John 16 Jesus says, "He will bring glory to me by taking from what is mine and making it known to you. All that belongs to the Father is mine. That is why I said the Spirit will take from what is mine and make it known to you" (vv. 14-15). Part of the job of the Holy Spirit is to make Jesus known to us. The Holy Spirit is not about bringing a new message of his own and he's not about bringing glory to himself. He's the spotlight who illuminates Jesus. Sometimes the Holy Spirit is called the shy member of the Trinity because he doesn't make a great fuss about himself—he testifies to Jesus.

And just as Jesus was a guide to his twelve disciples, so the Holy Spirit will be a guide to all of Jesus' followers. Jesus says, "but when he, the Spirit of truth, comes, he will guide you into all truth" (John 16:13). If you look closely at this verse, you'll see that the Spirit guides his followers into all truth by speaking what he hears from Jesus, not by speaking on his own. The Holy Spirit taught the apostles all things and reminded them of everything Jesus said to them. The apostles passed that on to us through their writings in the New Testament. And the Holy Spirit continues to remind us, teach us and guide us into all things because he continues to remind us and teach us about Jesus.

And the interesting thing is that Jesus could only really be with twelve disciples in one place at the one time. But because the Holy Spirit is God's Spirit living within our own spirits, he can be in every believer, across every age, in every place. I reckon that's what Jesus meant when he said, "It is for your good that I am going away", because the Spirit can be the presence of Jesus for all followers in a way that Jesus could be only for a few. The Spirit really takes over that particular role of Jesus, now that Jesus has left this world to be at the right hand of the Father in heaven. As Jesus comforted his disciples, so the Spirit comforts us. As Jesus testified to God, so the Spirit testifies to Jesus. As Jesus was misunderstood and rejected, so too will the Spirit be misunderstood and rejected. "The world cannot accept him, because it neither sees him nor knows him" (John 14:17). But Christians know him because he lives in us.

Keep the connection
Now, what does all this mean for us? Because Jesus was the man

of the Spirit in his lifetime, and because he is the giver of the Spirit since he left the world, there is an unbreakable and close connection between Jesus and the Holy Spirit. This helps us work through some of the confusing things we hear about the Holy Spirit from other Christians.

If the Spirit's job is to testify to Jesus—to make Jesus' life and teaching known to us—then we cannot and should not expect him to give us a new message of his own. So it's a mistake to connect any teaching to the Holy Spirit if it does not shed light upon Jesus in some way. Remember, the Spirit is the spotlight that shines upon Jesus. The focus is not on the Spirit himself; the focus, the attention, the limelight is on Jesus, and particularly on what Jesus has done for us in dying for us and rising again. In the same way, if the Spirit's job is to make Jesus known to us, then we cannot claim that a religious or spiritual experience is from the Spirit if it does not line up with the life of Jesus.

It can be confusing when some churches seem obsessed with the Holy Spirit, wanting to make him (the shy member of the Trinity) the centre of attention. It is even more confusing when there does not seem to be any connection to Jesus. It is confusing and damaging when people get caught up with so-called spiritual experiences that have no connection to Jesus. In the day to day of my job I hear stories about churches in which strange things happen. I have heard of people laughing uncontrollably, of people making animal noises; I've even heard of gold dust falling from the ceiling of a church. These are all allegedly from the Holy Spirit but they have no connection to Jesus. To be completely honest, I just don't think they are from the Holy Spirit—not because God cannot cause gold dust or any other kind of dust to fall from the ceiling, but because gold dust is not connected to the message or life of Jesus.

Other churches create a church or 'worship' experience that's really emotion-charged so that everyone can 'feel' the Holy Spirit—you have this intense emotional experience and 'feel' the Holy Spirit. But it's worth remembering that the Holy Spirit is a person, not an emotion. You *feel* an emotion—and I'm not saying there's anything wrong with that—but you *know* a person. In John's Gospel, Jesus doesn't talk about *feeling* the Holy Spirit; he talks about *knowing* him. Jesus says we'll know him because he'll teach us about Jesus.

You might think I'm being critical of certain types of churches like charismatic or Pentecostal churches. But I think there's just as much opportunity for error in more reformed or conservative churches. In some reformed or conservative churches you could be mistaken for thinking that the most important thing is to be right. But being spiritual is not about just being right. There is absolutely no point in claiming that any teaching or experience we have is from the Holy Spirit if it does not move us towards the kind of life that Jesus lived. Even in my own church I worry that I talk, people listen, but nothing changes. Or people read but nothing changes. Or people learn but nothing changes. I can find nowhere in Jesus' life or teaching where he said it's all about what you know and it doesn't matter if nothing changes. If what we hear about Jesus, if what we read, if what we learn makes no difference to our lives, then that knowledge is not from the Holy Spirit and we are kidding ourselves.

If we want the Holy Spirit to be at work in our lives then we need to keep our eyes firmly on Jesus, because it's Jesus to whom all the Spirit's witness and focus and attention is directed. So as you continue to learn about Jesus, as the Holy Spirit shines his light on Jesus in the pages of the Bible, don't be fooled that it's all about what you know or about being right. Make sure that what you learn moves you and changes you to be more like Jesus.

CHAPTER 3

The Holy Spirit and mission

If you had to choose between having a comfortable life and having an adventurous life, which would you choose? When the choice is as stark as that, many of us would choose adventure over comfort. Adventure just sounds more... well, adventurous and interesting. Adventure sounds like an overseas holiday, whereas comfort sounds like a weekend in your pyjamas. Adventure sounds like Indiana Jones; comfort sounds like your old English teacher marking essays by the fire. Adventure just sounds like more fun.

Basically, when the Holy Spirit is first given to Christians in the book of Acts, he sends them on an adventure. Jesus described the Holy Spirit as a Counsellor or Comforter, but when the Holy Spirit is first given to the believers they are thrust into a gripping adventure rather than being wrapped up in a snuggly spiritual blanket. The Spirit is less about bringing personal comfort and more about sending us out on a mission. So in this chapter we are going to discover how the Holy Spirit is at work in the church's great task of spreading the good news of Jesus to the ends of the earth.

The Holy Spirit begins the mission

In Acts 1, after his resurrection, Jesus instructed the disciples to stay in Jerusalem to "receive power when the Holy Spirit comes… [to] be my witnesses in Jerusalem, and in all Judea and Samaria, and to the ends of the earth" (v. 8). Then at the beginning of Acts 2, on a day known as the Day of Pentecost, something extraordinary happened when the Holy Spirit came upon the believers in Jerusalem. A violent wind blew, and what looked like little flames of fire rested above each of Jesus' followers. It evidently made quite a noise and was quite a sight because a crowd gathered, and as it turns out it was a multicultural crowd because there were Jews there "from every nation under heaven" (Acts 2:5).

But then an even more extraordinary thing took place. When the Holy Spirit came upon Jesus' disciples, they all started to speak the good news about Jesus in the various native languages of the people in the crowd. These were languages that the disciples did not normally speak. The crowd was filled with people from every nation under heaven, and Jesus' followers started miraculously speaking in every language under heaven so that the people in the crowd could understand the message about Jesus in their own language. Naturally, the crowd was amazed. And, as always, there were also cynics and sceptics and doubters and haters about, who basically accused Jesus' followers of being as drunk as skunks.

That might sound like a nasty accusation, but it actually gave the apostle Peter an opportunity to stand before everyone and preach the gospel with great authority. So Peter preached about Jesus' miracles, about his death and especially about his resurrection, and concluded his speech with these words:

> "Therefore let all Israel be assured of this: God has made this Jesus, whom you crucified, both Lord and Christ."
>
> When the people heard this, they were cut to the heart and said to Peter and the other apostles, "Brothers, what shall we do?" (Acts 2:36-37)

On that very first day, 3000 people turned to Jesus (Acts 2:41). The Holy Spirit is about mission. He jump-started evangelism from the moment he was first given to all of Jesus' followers in Jerusalem. And when the believers immediately met with persecution and derision, the Holy Spirit used that difficult situation as an opportunity for further evangelism, as Peter authoritatively preached the word of God to the gathered crowd.

The Holy Spirit continues the mission

You could be tempted to think that the Day of Pentecost, the first time that the Holy Spirit was given, was a one-off. And in many ways it was. Yet that first day set the course for the mission work of the Holy Spirit, which is described as the book of Acts continues. Time and again you see the Spirit moving followers of Jesus to proclaim him boldly. This first happened in Jerusalem in Acts 2. But true to Jesus' prediction, it continued, moving from Jerusalem out through Judea and into Samaria by the beginning of Acts 8. After great persecution in Jerusalem the believers were scattered and preached the word of God wherever they were scattered. As the Word was preached, men and women turned to Christ. And the Spirit was given to those who believed so that new converts would keep the mission rolling on.

In the next couple of chapters of Acts, two exceptional spiritual events happened—events that would open up the preaching of the good news about Jesus into the Gentile world. Firstly, Saul of

Damascus—who was responsible in some ways for starting the persecution that scattered the believers out from Jerusalem in the first place (Acts 8:1, 9:1)—was radically converted to the faith (Acts 9). He was busily arresting Christians until the resurrected Jesus blinded him with a brilliant light from heaven and personally confronted him. He became a follower of Jesus, and was filled with the Holy Spirit and then given the special charge of carrying the name of Jesus before the Gentiles as well as the people of Israel (Acts 9:15).

Secondly, the apostle Peter—who had so boldly proclaimed Jesus in Jerusalem—was given a strange vision involving all kinds of animals and reptiles and birds and a blanket. You might want to read it for yourself in Acts 10. But the long and the short of it is that as he interacted with a great God-fearing non-Jewish dude called Cornelius, Peter learned—slowly, as was the usual way with him—that the good news about Jesus was for Gentiles as well as for Jews. And he learned that the Holy Spirit was a gift for Gentiles as well as for Jews. So by the end of the tenth chapter of Acts, the Holy Spirit had driven the mission of getting the good news about Jesus from Jerusalem into Judea and Samaria and then outside Israel into all the world.

The Spirit and the miraculous

There are a couple of interesting things to say quickly about the Holy Spirit and the start of the mission. The most visible or noticeable things that seemed to happen as the first people became Christians were miraculous things like healings and speaking in tongues (later on we'll talk about what 'tongues' means). Some folks think this means that speaking in tongues and miraculous healings should happen today every time someone becomes a Christian by the work of the Holy Spirit.

But here's the thing: if you look more closely at the book of Acts and read a bit further into the book, and if you read the rest of the New Testament, you discover that only on quite rare occasions did miraculous things happen when people became Christians. And it's much the same these days. Occasionally, as people receive the good news about Jesus by the power of the Holy Spirit, some outwardly extraordinary things might happen (like a healing). But most of the time this does not happen. Most of the time there is just the 'ordinary' miracle of a sinful person having their sins forgiven and their life turned around by the power of God!

The Spirit and the Word

It is also interesting to see that the preaching of God's word is always present with the mission of the Holy Spirit in the book of Acts. This means that if there is anything to expect or look for as the gospel goes out into the world, it is the preaching of the word about Jesus. Perhaps this should not surprise us. If the Holy Spirit was at work with the word of God at the beginning of creation, then it makes sense that the Holy Spirit continues to be at work with the word of God in making new creations out of men and women as they receive the message of the gospel by the light of the Spirit.

The Holy Spirit equips us for mission

I am guessing that by this stage, you can see that the way the Holy Spirit drove the mission for evangelism at the start of Christianity was through the apostles. Perhaps you think that is just because those guys were Christian superheroes. People like the apostle Peter and the apostle Paul were superstars of the faith; they'll probably have their own room or even their own castle in heaven. But to think that is to actually miss what happens in the book of Acts—and throughout Christian history since then, for that matter. Because the further you go into Christian history—from the time of Jesus, through the time of Acts, all the way up till now—the more you realize that the good news about Jesus didn't spread towards the ends of the earth because of a tiny band of superhero Christians like Peter and Paul. You realize that in fact the gospel has been spread by millions of ordinary Christians who have been equipped for the task by the extraordinary Holy Spirit. So it is not just that the Holy Spirit takes the initiative in getting the mission going. He also equips men and women everywhere to testify to Jesus.

You can grasp the connection between the Holy Spirit and human testimony about Jesus in Acts 1, as we've already seen, where the resurrected Lord Jesus tells the disciples that they will "receive power when the Holy Spirit comes on you; and you will be my witnesses in Jerusalem, and in all Judea and Samaria, and to the ends of the earth" (v. 8). How were those first disciples going to be witnesses to Jesus in Jerusalem? It had something to do with having the empowering presence of the Holy Spirit within them. He is the one who teaches his people the right thing to say at the right time (Luke 12:11-12). The equipping work of the Holy Spirit for the task of testifying to Jesus certainly empowered the apostles, whom Jesus had chosen while he was here.

But think about it for a bit: there were only eleven of them at this stage (since Judas Iscariot had killed himself after betraying Jesus). How could eleven of them possibly make it to the ends of the earth? Only ten chapters later there is another apostle—Paul, who was not even a follower of Jesus in Acts 1—witnessing to Jesus throughout the non-Jewish world. So Jesus' urging of the apostles to be witnesses to Christ in the power of the Holy Spirit must be a command that goes beyond the mere eleven of them.

Have you ever wondered who will be a witness of the resurrected and ascended Lord Jesus to the woman who runs on the treadmill next to you at the gym every Tuesday morning? Or to your mate in class? Or to the person who's not really your buddy but who could really use a buddy? Or to your teacher? Or to your clients and customers? Or to your staff or business partners? Or to your boss? Because I don't think it's going to be the apostle Peter, or the apostle John, or even the apostle Paul. It's probably going to be you, isn't it? It will be just ordinary Christians like you and me who—with the power of the Holy Spirit—take the good news of Jesus to whichever end of the earth we happen to be living in.

And as it turns out, the task of witnessing for Jesus is an urgent one—much more urgent than we think. As Jesus is whisked up to heaven in a cloud, the disciples stand "looking intently up into the sky" (Acts 1:10). Which is so understandable, humanly speaking. I mean, I get a little thrill every time I drive past the airport—so much so that I'll often opt to travel to the south side of Sydney (where the airport is) through the city, despite $8 in tolls, because I love seeing the planes take off into the sky and watching until they disappear from view. So it's very human for the apostles to gaze at the spectacle of a *man* ascending to the sky. And you cannot help but feel a little sorry for them when two angels—you can tell that they're angels by their dress and their message—give them a dressing down:

> "Men of Galilee," they said, "why do you stand here looking into the sky? This same Jesus, who has been taken from you into heaven, will come back in the same way you have seen him go into heaven." (Acts 1:11)

In recording this moment, Luke emphasizes the fact that Jesus went up into the sky; he repeats the phrase "into the sky" or "into heaven" four times in two verses. Jesus went into the sky, into heaven; but what the angels are saying is that looking up there is not going to bring him back. "Why do you stand here looking up at the sky? You've got to go from Jerusalem to the ends of the earth with the message of Jesus. And you might as well start now. Look out, boys, not up!" This seems to be the flavour of what the angels are saying. There's an urgency to the task of witnessing to Jesus. Even as he's ascending to heaven the apostles are told to get on with it. So there's also work for us to do as, armed with the Holy Spirit, we urgently get on with the task of witnessing and testifying to Jesus in a world that desperately needs to hear the good news about him.

The Holy Spirit convicts people's hearts in mission

Perhaps the last question, then, is how does the Spirit work in people when we talk to them about Jesus? If it's true that one of the things we are supposed to do now that Jesus is in heaven is to witness to him, and if the Holy Spirit not only began the mission but continues to drive it forward, how does the Holy Spirit work to turn people to Jesus? This is a vitally important question to answer, because ultimately it provides us with hope that our feeble words and weak attempts are not all that's going on when we are evangelizing family and friends.

We have already cherry-picked some verses from Jesus' teaching about the Spirit in John 14-16, and seen how the Holy Spirit is a guide and comfort to all of Jesus' disciples. In John 16, Jesus explains that it's for the good of his disciples that he is going back to heaven:

> "It is for your good that I am going away. Unless I go away, the Counsellor will not come to you; but if I go, I will send him to you. When he comes, he will convict the world of guilt in regard to sin and righteousness and judgement: in regard to sin, because men do not believe in me..." (John 16:7-9)

Since Jesus has now returned to heaven, the Holy Spirit has come, and one of the things he is doing is convicting the world of guilt in regard to sin, righteousness and judgement. These verses are pretty tricky to get your head around, and decent Christian thinkers have come up with a variety of possible understandings. However, it seems like Jesus is saying that without the Holy Spirit working in the hearts of people, they would have no idea of the desperately dangerous place in which they find themselves. They are guilty but they need the Spirit to show them their guilt. He impresses the guilt that belongs to the whole world on to the consciences of individual sinners. He convicts the hearts of sinful people so that they understand their need for Christ. And then he moves in their hearts so that they might accept the righteousness that comes not from themselves but from what Jesus has done for them on the cross.

We tend to think that being convicted of guilt and judgement and things like that is really negative. But actually it is among the very kindest of things that God does for people through his Spirit. Imagine being in a safari park with all the African animals cruising around doing their African animal thing. You're cruising around and through them, enjoying getting up close and personal with such amazing creatures. But without realizing it, you have just moved into the gap between a mother elephant and her baby. If a park ranger happened to be there to warn you of the danger and to guide you towards safety, would he be doing you a kindness or a disservice? Given how dangerous it is to be between a mother and a baby elephant, I think we can agree that the park ranger would be providing a very helpful service. Likewise, when the Holy Spirit convicts people of sin and judgement because of their unbelief, he is providing the ultimate service of revealing a danger they are otherwise ignorant of. Then he drives them to a place of safety, to the very foot of the cross of Christ, where Jesus died so that we might be counted as righteous in him.

If evangelism was just about our feeble words and best attempts, the mission of Jesus would be in trouble. But because the Holy Spirit takes the initiative in driving it forward—from Jerusalem to the ends of the earth—and because he equips ordinary people to speak true words, and because he convicts the hearts of sinners of their great need for Jesus, the mission powers on. The question is whether or not we want to partner with him in this urgent task. The Holy Spirit is sometimes called the Comforter, but he's not about bringing us a safe and cozy life. He is asking us to join him on an adventure to take the message of salvation in Jesus to the ends of the earth. So unless you would rather be like an English teacher marking essays by the fire, it's time to get on board with that mission.

From here we will start to look at how the Holy Spirit works in our Christian lives, not just at the start but all the way through until we see Jesus face to face in heaven.

CHAPTER 4

The Spirit in our Christian lives

As we saw in the last chapter, when the apostles preached the good news about Jesus in the earliest days of Christianity, the Holy Spirit convicted the hearts of many people to turn from their sins back to God in light of Jesus' life, death and resurrection. In this chapter we'll look at how the Holy Spirit works at the start of the Christian life, as well as how he continues to work in us for the rest of our Christian lives.

The Spirit kicks off the Christian life

The way we usually talk about the start of the Christian life, you could be forgiven for thinking that it was pretty much like going to lunch at the local buffet restaurant. You know, the sort of place where you pay a price that seems pretty reasonable on the way in. There's a salad bar and a pasta station with four kinds of rapidly cooling pasta and three kinds of lukewarm pasta sauce, each quickly developing its own batch of bacteria. A few other tepid dishes swim around in warming trays. You choose whatever you want and eat until you're almost sick (thinking to yourself on the way out that the price doesn't seem so reasonable any more). That's the whole deal with buffets: you choose from all the available dishes what you want to eat and how much you want to eat. It's all about your choice.

And that's generally how people describe starting off in the Christian life. We think that becoming a Christian is basically about us making a decision or choice to follow Jesus. We think it's about *us* choosing to respond to what Jesus has done for us. Among all the religious and spiritual options on offer, we choose Jesus. But that's not how the New Testament describes the process at all. For a fuller description of how God's will and our human choices work together in salvation and the Christian life, you can read the Little Black Book called *Predestination*. But for now we are simply going to note that, rather than the start of your Christian life just being about your decision or choice or response to Jesus, in actual fact the Holy Spirit is intimately involved in the process.

In John 3, Jesus has a conversation with a religious Jewish guy called Nicodemus. In the Gospel accounts, the Jewish religious officials are usually hostile and opposed to Jesus. But it appears that Nicodemus sees something in Jesus that makes him want to find out more. Of course, Nicodemus is still afraid of the other Jewish religious guys so he catches Jesus at night, when there's much less chance of being seen. They start talking about being "born again", which is another way of describing being saved or starting the Christian life:

> In reply Jesus declared, "I tell you the truth, no-one can see the kingdom of God unless he is born again."
>
> "How can a man be born when he is old?" Nicodemus asked. "Surely he cannot enter a second time into his mother's womb to be born!"
>
> Jesus answered, "I tell you the truth, no-one can enter the kingdom of God unless he is born of water and the Spirit. Flesh gives birth to flesh, but the Spirit gives birth to spirit. You should not be surprised at my saying, 'You must be born again'. The wind blows wherever it pleases. You hear its sound, but you cannot tell where it comes from or where it is going. So it is with everyone born of the Spirit." (John 3:3-8)

It's one of those intriguing little conversations that Jesus often seems to have, in which people don't quite understand what he's talking about. It must have been pretty frustrating for Jesus. He's talking about entering the kingdom of God, and he says that entry into this kingdom means being born again. Perhaps understandably, Nicodemus thinks it's a bit unlikely that he's going to be able to crawl back into his mother's womb, now that he's a big fella and all. So Jesus has to spell out to Nicodemus that being "born again" is a spiritual concept, not a physical one. Flesh gives birth to flesh, but Jesus has spiritual birth on his mind. He is saying that you need a spiritual birth to enter the kingdom of God, to be saved, to become a Christian. A person must be born again by water, which is a reference to the cleansing of sin. And a person must be born again by the Spirit; you cannot enter the kingdom of God in any other way. Notice how little he says about us choosing Jesus like we might choose spaghetti alfredo at the pasta bar.

If being born again by the Spirit sounds mysterious, that seems to be the point as Jesus then talks about the wind blowing. And if you think about it for a moment, Jesus is on to something. When the wind blows we cannot see where it comes from. Meteorologists would probably tell you that it has something to do with high and low pressure systems. And little children might tell you that the wind comes from the trees, because they see the trees blowing and simply connect the dots—the trees are bending so they must cause the wind. But both groups miss the point.

When you see the wind blowing, it's a bit mysterious. You know it's blowing but you don't know what makes it blow or where it comes from. The Holy Spirit is equally mysterious; the way he works is beyond our understanding (although thankfully it's not beyond God's sovereign control). The Holy Spirit will have his way in our lives; he will bring forth spiritual birth in whomever he pleases. It's all about *his* choice, not ours, and the truth is that we might find his choices and workings pretty surprising.

You just cannot read the conversation between Jesus and Nicodemus without realizing that our salvation is more about something God does in us than about something we do. Without doubt, the Holy Spirit is intimately involved in the beginning of our Christian lives.

The Spirit works all through the Christian life

As it turns out, the Holy Spirit is intimately involved in *all* of the Christian life—not just the beginning. And this is no surprise if you consider the physical life of a human. After you're born, you don't immediately get on with things on your own. It's not as if you swim around in your mother's womb for a lazy nine months, then—following a fair bit of pushing and squeezing—out you pop ready to fend for yourself. Human life doesn't work like that. Not even the animal world works like that. The chicks stay in the nest waiting for the mother bird to bring back some worms, the cubs hang around the lioness, and the calves suckle from their mother cows. There might be some creatures like mosquitoes that know how to be annoying pretty much straight away. But we humans are highly dependent on our parents for years after we're born. They give us life, wipe our butts, teach us to walk, take us to school, cook us our food, pay for our braces, take us on holidays, drive us everywhere, and pay for everything. And even if we make it to the point of leaving home (which is a big "if" these days), they remain in most cases the biggest influences in our lives, for better or worse. It's not like once you're out of the womb, you're on your own.

If the Holy Spirit is intimately involved at the beginning of the Christian life, it makes sense that he remains involved throughout the Christian life. The real question is, in what ways does he work in our Christian lives?

Live by the Spirit

The New Testament teaches us that the Holy Spirit works in us to make us more like Jesus as we continue in the Christian life. What does the Holy Spirit want to do in our lives after we are born again? He wants to make us more like Jesus. That's the key idea in Galatians 5, where the apostle Paul tells us to live by the Spirit:

> So I say, walk by the Spirit, and you will not gratify the desires of the flesh. For the flesh desires what is contrary to the Spirit, and the Spirit what is contrary to the flesh. (Gal 5:16-17)

Here we see again the New Testament's contrast of the ideas of Spirit and flesh. But when the apostle Paul uses the word 'flesh' here, he's not just talking about human flesh or human bodies. He's got in mind something a little different. What he really means is that which is earthly and opposed to God. 'Flesh' describes humans in their opposite-ness to God and in their opposition to God. It's talking about people who haven't been born again by the Spirit. So Galatians is really urging us not to walk (that is, live) like unbelieving humans who are opposed to God and whose ways are opposed to God's ways. Instead, we are told that once we have been born again by the Spirit, we are to go on living by the Spirit.

We are also told that if we live by the Spirit we will not gratify the desires of the flesh. Or to put it positively, if we walk by the Spirit we will live a life that looks increasingly like the life of Jesus. "Walk by the Spirit" is the command; if you do that, you will not live according to the flesh as though you were still a part of humanity opposed to God. You will look more like Jesus and less like the person you were before you became a Christian.

Obviously, we need to understand what it means to walk (or live) by the Spirit. To live by the Spirit is to let your life, your choices, your actions, your thoughts, your words, your attitudes and your habits be governed by God rather than by desires that are opposed to God; desires you had before you were born again by the Holy Spirit.

In most of the situations we face in daily life it's not all that tricky working out what "the flesh" desires. And as we continue in the Christian life, growing in our understanding of all that Jesus has done for us, it becomes clearer and clearer what he wants us to be. We come to Jesus as we are, but he doesn't want us to just stay as we are. He loves us too much for that and he has much better things in mind for us. So to live by the Spirit means to put into practice what God wants for us, rather than what we might have wanted before we became Christians. It means increasingly saying to God, "No part of my life is off limits, no part of my week is off limits, no part of my future is off limits". And then the Holy Spirit will shape us in every part of our lives to be more like Jesus, who perfectly put into practice what God wanted for him.

Fight by the Spirit

You don't have to think about it very long before you realize that the Spirit's shaping of us is going to involve a fight. Listen to how the apostle Paul talks about it:

> For the flesh desires what is contrary to the Spirit, and the Spirit what is contrary to the flesh. They are in conflict with each other, so that you do not do what you want. (Gal 5:17)

The conflict between the Spirit and the flesh can result in you not doing the Jesus-thing you want to do, but the sinful or 'fleshy' thing you do not want to do. This might cause you some frustration and confusion. You might wonder why you still battle with sin even though Jesus died for you and defeated sin, death and the devil. But that's because the temptation to think, live, speak and act like we did before we were born again remains. When we become

Christians, we are saved from the *penalty* of our sin because Jesus took that penalty in our place on the cross. In heaven we will be saved from the *presence* of sin because the devil will be utterly destroyed and we will be perfected. In the meantime we are being saved from the *power* of sin, but that's an ongoing process because sin remains very real in our lives. That's why there is conflict and that's why we need to take seriously the command to live by the Spirit.

But if you feel like you aren't strong enough, or you're too tired or confused to fight against the worldly desires of the flesh, there is great news for you. The first bit of great news is that the power of God the Holy Spirit is available to you in this fight.

You'd be out of touch if you hadn't noticed that gaming is a pretty big deal these days. It's now a bigger industry than the film industry. And it's not like it's only teenage boys playing— the average age of gamers is well beyond the teenage years. Many people are familiar with the *Call of Duty* or *Assassin's Creed* or *Halo* kinds of games, where you control a character (like a soldier) on the screen. You tell your little on-screen soldier-self to put down the pistol and pick up the bazooka, to throw the grenade or to eat the grenade, to stab the enemy or to dance with the enemy, to jump in the helicopter or to blow up the helicopter. The little on-screen character is not on his own; he has all the skill and power and influence and control of the gamer at his disposal.

Similarly, in the fight against the temptation to live like we did before we became Christians, we have the influence of the Holy Spirit at our disposal; we are not on our own. Through the words of Scripture we know what to do. Because the Holy Spirit lives within our own spirits, we have the power to put those words of Scripture into practice. This means that in any situation we can say "No" to sin and "Yes" to Jesus, "Yes" to living by the Spirit. The power and control of God the Holy Spirit is available so that we never *have* to lose the fight against our sinful desires.

The second bit of good news is that it's actually easy to work out when the battle is raging. It's not like we have to think really hard to work out if we're giving in to the flesh. The signs are obvious, which is exactly what Paul says:

> The acts of the flesh are obvious: sexual immorality, impurity and debauchery, idolatry and witchcraft; hatred, discord, jealousy, fits of rage, selfish ambition, dissensions, factions and envy; drunkenness, orgies, and the like. I warn you, as I did before, that those who live like this will not inherit the kingdom of God. (Gal 5:19-21)

When you give in to the desires of the flesh, the results—or what the apostle Paul here calls the "acts of the flesh"—are obvious. If you find yourself involved in sexual immorality, playing around with witchcraft, hatred, violent anger, divisions and drunkenness, they are obvious signs you are living according to the flesh rather than by the Spirit. They are clear signs that you are not letting the Holy Spirit control and influence you so that you become more like Jesus. They are signs that you are living like you are not a Christian. So it is good to keep going back to that list and asking yourself whether there is any area of life—selfish attitudes, hateful words, immoral actions—in which you're not living by the Spirit. Is there an area of life that you need to give control of to the Holy Spirit who lives in you? That's a good question to ask yourself regularly if you are going to let the Spirit be at work in your life.

The fruit of the Spirit

Living by the Spirit involves a fight, but it also produces fruit. In other words, just as the signs of living according to the flesh are obvious, so too are the signs of living by the Spirit. This is because living by the Spirit produces fruit in our lives.

Autumn and winter can be pretty slow times when it comes

to fruit—there's usually just a few scabby apples and sloppy pears about. But come the spring and summer months it's like Fruitopia; there's fruit everywhere. Beautiful fruit: fat plump peaches, tangy cherries, juicy mangoes, bright red strawberries. My mouth waters just thinking about it. And if you ever go to an orchard (because fruit doesn't actually grow at the supermarket) and you have a look at fruit trees in full bloom, it's about as pretty a sight as you'll ever see. It just looks good. Plenty of fruit on the outside means the tree is healthy inside. Good things, not bad things, are at work in the tree. The fruit you can see on the outside indicates health on the inside. And it's like that when we live by the Spirit, so says Paul:

> But the fruit of the Spirit is love, joy, peace, patience, kindness, goodness, faithfulness, gentleness and self-control… (Gal 5:22-23)

When we live by the Spirit it produces fruit in our lives. It produces love, joy, peace, patience, kindness, goodness, faithfulness, gentleness and self-control. But it's not really like you can choose which fruit to put in your spiritual hamper. You probably noticed that it does not say, "the *fruits* of the Spirit *are*"; it says, "the *fruit* of the Spirit *is*". In other words, the point is not that you will only see some of these things forming in your life so you should choose the three that come most naturally. The point is that you will see all these together—one fruit—develop in your life if you live by the Spirit; if you let him control your thoughts, attitudes, words and actions; if you say to him, "There is no part of my life that is off limits. I want to become more like Jesus in every part of my life."

So, again, have a look at that list because it might help you to see the areas of your life that you find easier to give over to the control of the Spirit. It might also help you to work out those parts of your life that you find more difficult to let the Holy Spirit shape.

Living by the Spirit means there is a fight on, but it also produces fruit in your life. And just look at how attractive that is in comparison to the acts of the flesh, which Galatians has just described. Why wouldn't you want to see the fruit of the Spirit in your life?

Keep in step with the Spirit
At the end of Galatians 5 we discover the part we need to play in response to the knowledge that the Holy Spirit is involved all through our Christian lives:

> Those who belong to Christ Jesus have crucified the flesh with its passions and desires. Since we live by the Spirit, let us keep in step with the Spirit. (Gal 5:24-25)

If you check out those two verses and compare them with verse 16, which we looked at earlier, you will see a stronger wording of the situation. Verse 16 urges us to live by the Spirit so that we won't give in to the desires of the flesh. Verse 24 tells us that as Christians we have *already* crucified the flesh. We've already put it to death; we've already declared that its passions and desires have no right to dictate how we live. That person who used to live in opposition to God is no longer alive; a new person who has been born of the Spirit and who walks by the Spirit is now alive. And if you have crucified or put to death the flesh, there is no reason to go back to living according to it. Verse 25 is also more strongly worded. It doesn't urge us to live by the Spirit as it did in verse 16; it assumes we *already* live by the Spirit, saying, "*Since* we live by the Spirit". So the instruction is: if you live by the Spirit, then keep in step with the Spirit. Keep walking with the Spirit and by the Spirit.

So there is a tension in how we live. On the one hand, it is true that because of what Jesus has done for us, we have put to death the flesh. We nailed those desires and the way of life that is opposed to God to the same cross that Jesus died on. They no longer master us; instead we are influenced and controlled and governed by the Spirit. But, on the other hand, as we live by the Spirit we determine whether we keep in step with him. We can choose obedience so that we walk in step with the Spirit and become more like Jesus; or we can choose to go back to our old ways, the ways of the flesh, and be the person we were before we knew God and were born again by his Spirit. Then, instead of becoming more like Jesus, we will stay as we are.

The Holy Spirit, who is involved in our conversion and who lives in us, is at work to make us more like Jesus—to produce his fruit of love, joy, peace and patience in our lives. But we have a major role to play, because it doesn't happen automatically. It happens as we discover parts of our life that need to be ruled by Jesus and we say, "Ok, you can have that part of me". It happens as we read Scripture and the Holy Spirit convicts us that what it says requires us to change in obedient response. It happens in a thousand different situations every day when we are faced with a choice to do or not to do, to say or not to say, to think or not to think, to believe or not to believe, and we feel that nudge of the

Spirit pushing us to do the right thing, to not say the hateful thing, to not harbour the evil thoughts, and to believe that what God says to us in Scripture is the very best thing for us. If you want to keep in step with the Spirit, let him have his way in every aspect of your life as he brings it up in Scripture or in your conscience.

Truly, as Christians we do live by the Spirit, having crucified the flesh. But if the Holy Spirit is going to have his way in our life, it will require us to fight to obey; to fight to surrender those parts of our lives to him that we want to run our own way; to fight to believe. Again and again, just as in Galatians 5, we see the qualities of Jesus being set before us as the very same qualities the Holy Spirit wants to produce in us. Ultimately, the issue is not about what the Spirit wants to do in our lives, but whether we are willing to let him have his way.

CHAPTER 5

The Holy Spirit and gifts

I'm a little bit of a history buff. I don't have an encyclopedic knowledge of historical events or anything like that, but I am a sucker for history documentaries. In World War II, the Allies (they're the good guys) commenced their final assault on the Nazis (the bad guys) in Europe in June 1944, on what would become known as D-Day. The Nazis were occupying France. In the steel mills of northern England the Allies had built these fat metal bridges, which their navy fleets towed across the English Channel under the cover of darkness and dropped off on the shores of Omaha beach and Arromanches in north-western France (the bridges are still there to this day; you can see them just off the coast). The Allied air force bombed the living daylights out of German artillery positions on the coast, and then the Allied army moved their tanks and trucks across the bridges that the navy had moved into position in the water. They stormed the beaches and swept through German positions in what was the decisive move to end the war in Europe. D-Day was an amazing show of unity, not just among Allied military forces but also between the military and industry. English steel mills as well as British, American and Canadian navies, air forces and armies were all working together for a common goal: the liberation and freedom of Europe from the Nazis.

It's a great picture of how good things can be achieved when people use their different capabilities for the common good. And the opposite is also true—it's amazing how little progress we make when we get lost in quarrelling and pride and disunity. As we think about how the Holy Spirit works in our church life together, and in particular about the gifts that God gives us by his Spirit to use in our fellowship, there is great potential for unity and growth. But sadly, the things of the Spirit also have an amazing potential to bring disunity and division amongst Christians. It happens all the time. It might have happened in your church; it has certainly happened in groups I have been involved with.

As it turns out, such divisions are not all that unexpected. In our Bibles we find that the issue and use of gifts was a controversial and divisive issue amongst the Corinthian church, way back in the years immediately after Jesus. So much so that the apostle Paul devoted three chapters to the issue in his first letter to the Corinthians. 1 Corinthians 12-14 are really about what it means to be 'spiritual', and how our use of gifts in church life is part of that.

From a united God, for a united people

It seems to me that the first thing we are supposed to know, if we are not going to be ignorant and foolish with our use of gifts, is that it is a united God—Father, Son and Holy Spirit—who gives them to Christians. As the apostle Paul starts his critique of the way the Corinthians were using their gifts, he says:

> There are different kinds of gifts, but the same Spirit. There are different kinds of service, but the same Lord. There are different kinds of working, but the same God works all of them in all men.
> (1 Cor 12:4-6)

We are naturally concerned about what gifts we might have been given and how we should use them, but it's interesting to see that the first thing the apostle Paul tells us is that the emphasis is not on the gifts themselves but on the united God who gives them. In fact, the phrase 'spiritual gifts', which is often used in English translations of 1 Corinthians 12-14, is not actually there in the original language. The passage talks about 'gifts' and it talks about 'spiritual matters' or 'spiritual things', but it doesn't talk about 'spiritual gifts'—a phrase that might lead us to think it is *only* the Holy Spirit who has anything to do with the gifts and how we use them.

Paul wants to emphasize that although there are different gifts, it is the one God—Father, Son and Spirit—who gives them. There is perfect unity between the Holy Spirit, the Lord Jesus and God the Father, who together work in all the different kinds of gifts and service seen in the church. The Spirit, the Son and the Father are united in giving gifts and opportunities to the people of God. It's not like the Holy Spirit works independently of the Father and Son in this area, off in the back shed coming up with tricks and ideas that the Father and Jesus don't really know much about, like some sort of mad professor in the family. A united God—Father, Son and Spirit—is at work in gifts we exercise in church.

And because these gifts are given by a united God, they are designed to work for the benefit of a united group of Christian people. They are designed to build the church, the people of God, together to make it stronger—much stronger than individual Christians could be on their own. But our natural human tendency to be selfish, and to divide over our differences rather than to unite over what we share, means that this building up of the group won't happen unless God's word shapes our thinking. Which is why we must hear the instruction that gifts are given to each Christian not for themselves but for the common good (1 Cor 12:7). They are not given to individuals to make those individuals look impressive, or to make them seem flashy, or even to make them appear more spiritual. They are given for the good of all the church.

I've noticed that Christmas decorations are going up in the shops earlier and earlier these days. Tinsel and trees are starting to pop up in the middle of October. I feel troubled by this, partly because it turns a great celebration of the coming of our Saviour into the world into a crass marketing drive. It also troubles me because of the strain that Christmas puts on families who struggle to afford it; Christmas costs a bomb. But the main thing that bothers me is that it means there is one thing all the kids and the shops know for certain: Christmas is not about Jesus. It's not even about families getting together. It's about presents. The shops don't put up their decorations in October because they want more than two months to remind people of the birth of Jesus. They want to maximize their sales. The tinsel is not up to remind families of how good it is to get together. The shops want to sell presents. And kids know that the focus is on the presents too because Christmas morning is the only morning of the year when they get up at 4 am to unwrap them. There is no doubt that the gifts are the focus of Christmas.

That's why it is interesting to note that when the united God gives his gifts, the focus is not so much on the gifts themselves, nor even on the person who has been given the gift. The focus is on the common good, and the benefit those gifts can provide to God's people. The Holy Spirit is not interested in making an individual look good or appear to be more spiritual than others. He works in us and equips us to do things for the benefit of others. And if Christians remembered this, there would be much less chance of this issue of gifts creating division rather than unity.

What is a gift?

So what are these "gifts" and how do you know which ones you have?

A number of places in the New Testament list various gifts. In Romans 12 and 1 Peter 4, the list includes things like prophecy, serving, teaching, contributing and leading. Apart from 'prophecy', these all sound pretty straightforward. (We'll look at prophecy in the appendix.)

In 1 Corinthians 12 (which I quoted above), the apostle Paul lists the gifts of wisdom, knowledge, and faith (which is most likely talking about an extra measure of faith to tackle particular challenges in the Christian life). He also lists the gifts of healing, miraculous powers and prophecy, as well as the ability to distinguish between spirits—that is, to know whether things are from God or from another source. And there is lastly the gift of speaking in "different kinds of tongues" or 'languages' (v. 10), which we're not too sure about. 'Tongues' may be the ability to speak in other languages so that people from different nations can understand you (as a bunch of the disciples did at Pentecost in Acts 2). Other people say that 'tongues' here in 1 Corinthians 12 is a kind of heavenly prayer language that's not readily understandable to our ears, but since Paul gives no description of what he means by 'tongues', we can't know whether this idea is right.

So if we put together what we learn from the different passages in the New Testament about 'gifts', it's not so hard to understand what a 'gift' is. It is simply an ability or talent or opportunity that God gives you. You can choose to leave it idle, use it selfishly, or put it to good use by loving and serving others. Sounds pretty simple.

What we also discover is that gifts can look quite extraordinary or very ordinary. "Miraculous powers" sounds pretty intense, and so does "speaking in different kinds of tongues" (whatever that means). But a message of wisdom or the gift of faith can seem pretty run of the mill. And when the apostle Paul mentions the gift of healing we naturally think of the way Jesus healed people miraculously, but there's no reason why it could not also include the way Christian doctors and nurses use their God-given talents to help people get better, even if that appears to be considerably less 'spiritual'.

In fact, there is a second list of gifts towards the end of 1 Corinthians 12 (vv. 28-30) that includes helping others and even the gift of administration, of being a good organizer. And as I've already pointed out, the other lists of gifts in Romans 12 and 1 Peter 4 include things such as serving, teaching, giving money, encouraging and leading. So if you look at *all* the gifts mentioned in the New Testament, many of them don't seem all that amazing. You may never have thought that the ability to organize people or coordinate events could be a gift given to you by God through his Spirit. You would not naturally think that something as routine as setting out chairs for a meeting or serving coffee could be considered a 'spiritual' thing to do. But it is.

In fact, that is Paul's big point in 1 Corinthians 12-14. If you really want to be Spirit-people, he is saying, then use whatever gifts you've been given to love other people, to serve them, to build them up in Jesus. That's the real evidence of the Spirit's presence: when otherwise selfish people (like us) are using the gifts God has given us not for our own pride or importance but for the sake of others.

Your gifts, my gifts

Now you might view a list of gifts like the one in 1 Corinthians 12:8-10 and think that you don't have any of those gifts. You might even be tempted to think that a lack of miraculous powers or being able to heal people means you are a second-class Christian. If I look down the list of gifts at the beginning of 1 Corinthians 12, I don't think I have any of them either. I don't have the gift of healing; I reckon that I usually make people feel worse. Even though I am first-aid trained, the solution I offer to just about every medical complaint is to drink more water and eat more fruit. If you have a headache, drink more water and eat more fruit. If you have a cold, drink more water and eat more fruit. If your leg needs to be amputated, I'm sticking with the water and fruit. So it's probably safe to say that I don't have the gift of healing. Likewise, I've been a Christian my whole life, as far as I can tell, but I have never spoken in a language other than English—whether an earthly one or a heavenly one. People sometimes struggle to understand what I'm saying but that's not a gift; it's just bad communication.

But that doesn't mean the Holy Spirit hasn't given me any gifts. It just means that my gifts are not on that particular list. Perhaps I have the gifts of teaching or helping others or administration that Paul mentions later on in 1 Corinthians 12. Perhaps you have those gifts. Perhaps your gifts include serving, encouraging, contributing to the needs of others, or even showing mercy, which are all listed in Romans 12. None of the lists of gifts in the New Testament is exhaustive. If you can't find what God has gifted you with in any particular passage, that's ok. It just means that your gifts aren't on that list.

So how do you find out which gifts you have? There are surveys around that are supposed to help you work out your 'spiritual gifting', but I don't think the New Testament ever encourages us to look in the mirror and try to work out whether we have this particular gift or that one. It simply tells us to use what God has gifted us to do for the sake of others. And how do you know if God has gifted you to do something? By having a go; by seeing a need and trying to meet it. Besides, a survey is probably not going to identify that you have the gift of serving coffee or setting out chairs. If you just take the opportunities that exist to contribute to the life of your church, you'll figure out soon enough what abilities, talents, capabilities and opportunities God has given you to use for his service and the service of his people. You won't find out that you can encourage people if you never speak; you won't find out that you can be generous if you never give; and you won't discover that you love to serve behind the scenes, or even up front, if you never get involved in the life of your church. So give things a go.

The one and only Spirit, backed by the Father and Son, has given many gifts to each and every Christian person. Some may look more spectacular than others, but what matters more than what they look like is that all of them are given for the common good of the group of believers, not to make any individual believer look good.

Nobody is any better or worse because of gifts
The next important thing we need to say is that nobody is any better or worse a Christian because of their particular gifts. Remember that the focus of gifts is not on the individual, nor on the gift, but on the common good of the group. The aim is unity and building up, not some kind of spiritual elitism that causes disunity.

Disunity was the problem back in Corinth—that's why Paul wrote 1 Corinthians 12-14. One person thought he was more spiritual because he had the more 'spiritual' looking gifts like speaking in tongues; another person thought she was worthless and that her gifts were unimportant because they appeared less important or spectacular. It is amazing how this exact problem has continued to plague churches to this day, as Christians with the more spectacular looking gifts think and claim that other Christians are in some ways inferior believers. But in 1 Corinthians the apostle Paul cracks them for both attitudes because the particular gifts you have, regardless of how spectacular or ordinary they appear, cannot make you any better or any worse than another Christian with a different gift.

For the sake of argument, imagine if I told you that I recently went to the cinema and I ripped out my eyeballs and put them on a chair in the front row because I wanted to get the best view. Then I sliced out my mouth and put it near the candy bar so that I could chomp away on my popcorn without disrupting others. And then I ripped off my ears and stuck them near the speakers to hear the movie with maximum clarity. And then I sucked out my brain and left it right in the middle to soak up the whole vibe. Perfect: my eyes could see the film, my ears could hear it, my tongue could taste the popcorn and my brain could take in the vibe. It's obviously unbelievable, but it's also unbelievably stupid because you know that unless those parts are working *together*, all I'm left with is a sliced up face.

But that idea of a sliced up, dismembered body is how the Bible pictures Christians who think they're more important than other Christians on account of their gifts. The apostle Paul, still in 1 Corinthians 12, tells us that there are many parts that make up a body, but the many parts all form *one* body. And it's the same with the body of Christ, the church of God's people. People have different gifts but they all form one body, so it makes no sense for gifts to cause division. It's stupid for one part of the body—one person with a particular gift—to think they don't need other people with other gifts. That's just as stupid as another person with their gift thinking they are not needed or that they have nothing to contribute. As the body of Christ, we each play a part. Unity is the aim and division shows that we have missed the point. There are different gifts, but they don't make the different parts unequal. I think this is terrific because it means we don't all have to be the same. We can have different gifts and even different personalities and that's fine, as long as we see ourselves united as one body, one group of Christians with one Spirit and one Lord Jesus. I also love the fact that this means we are all needed. Our world tells us that people who seem less significant or important really *are* less significant and important. But in the church we are all needed. Nobody has all the gifts, and everybody has some. Nobody is better or worse off because of his or her gifts. Our gifts might be different, but all are needed because together we form the body of Christ.

This is great news indeed. However, I think it's still worth saying a few things about three particular gifts—the gift of tongues, the gift of prophecy and the gift of healing—because they are often the source of conflict and controversy among Christians. It's worth looking at them a little more closely in the hope that greater clarity from the Scriptures might bring greater unity. You can find this discussion in the appendix at the back of the book.

Love is the most excellent way

At the end of the day, whatever you decide about some of the more spectacular and controversial gifts, the most excellent way to use any gift is always the way of love. You may have read 1 Corinthians 13 before and thought that it was talking about love between a man and a woman, or even between two friends. But it's talking about how people in church—different parts of the body—use their gifts to benefit the body as a whole.

So if you think you already know which gift the Holy Spirit has given you, then make sure you use that gift in love for the benefit of the whole group. And if you think you have nothing to offer, then get involved in serving where there is opportunity and you will discover your gifting. But again, do this in love with an attitude of service that seeks the good of others. If you are aware of your gifts but do not put them to use because of fear or laziness, then love will push you to get more involved in the life of your fellowship so that the gifts God has given you can benefit others. You have to remember that when it comes to gifts, they are not about you. They are about us together. They are about the common good. They are from a united God for a united people.

Conclusion

We can't complete our little expedition into the person and work of the Holy Spirit without looking into the future. And our Bibles tell us that the Holy Spirit is the one who assures us that we already *are* a part of God's kingdom, and that we will enjoy our place in the kingdom for all eternity. Twice in 2 Corinthians (1:22, 5:5) and a further time in Ephesians 1:14, the apostle Paul tells us that the Holy Spirit is like a deposit, guaranteeing what is to come. When you pay an amount of money as a deposit for a car or a house or a holiday, that deposit gives you certainty that you will soon be enjoying whatever it is—car, house, holiday—in all its fullness. In the case of the deposit of the Holy Spirit, poured into our hearts by God himself, we have a 100% certain guarantee that we belong to God now and will enjoy perfect fellowship with him forever. What a great hope, and a great gift.

The magnificent Holy Spirit is not like a puny ghost at all. He is no-one less than God, and nothing less than one of the personal members of the Godhead alongside the Father and the Son. He does nothing less than open our eyes to see Jesus, connecting our spirits and hearts to Jesus, and shaping our lives to be more like Jesus. And then finally the Holy Spirit guarantees our place next to Jesus in God's eternal kingdom. What a great hope, and a great gift.

APPENDIX

Tongues, prophecy and healing

Of all the gifts listed in the New Testament, the gifts of tongues, prophecy and healing seem to cause the most controversy amongst modern-day Christians. So it's worth having a brief look at what the Bible says about them. You might even be surprised by how little it says about these gifts given the amount of attention they sometimes receive.

The gift of tongues

In chapter 5 when we were thinking about how a person's gifts make them neither better nor worse as a Christian, you may have noticed I didn't say that all gifts are equal. Although all gifts are valuable and to be valued in the church, Paul says in 1 Corinthians

12:31 that we should "eagerly desire the greater gifts". In other words, he must think that some gifts are better than others. This is a strange thing for Paul to say just after he's been arguing that gifts should not lead to division within the body of Christ (v. 25), and that each part of the body should have equal concern for each other. How then can some gifts be better than others?

It's not because some people are better than others, or because some gifts are more spectacular than others, but because some gifts do more good in the church than others. If love is to be our guide—and in 1 Corinthians 13 Paul insists it should be—then in love we should seek to exercise those gifts which most build up people in Jesus.

And that's what Paul goes on to say in chapter 14. He says that prophecy is a greater gift than tongues because with the gift of prophecy a person can speak words that strengthen, encourage and comfort other Christians (v. 3), whereas no-one understands someone who speaks in tongues. The one who speaks in tongues edifies (or builds up) himself because he is the only one who understands what he's saying, but the one who prophesies builds up the whole church. Paul makes it explicit in verse 5 when he says that the one who prophesies is greater, not because of the individual, but simply because the gift is useful not only to the individual (as in tongues), but to the whole gathering of people. He emphasizes this point in verse 12 when he says, "Since you are eager to have spiritual gifts [literally, 'to be spiritual'], try to excel in gifts that build up the church". And in verse 19 when he says, "But in the church I would rather speak five intelligible words to instruct others than ten thousand words in a tongue", he is not saying that speaking in tongues is bad, although it certainly led to pretty bad habits in Corinth! He wants the Corinthian Christians (and us) to understand that the true mark of the Holy Spirit's presence is not an intense and spectacular display of giftedness, but a heart that wants to love other people and build them up.

And this should not surprise us, since 'love' is the fruit of the Spirit.

The gift of prophecy

So now we understand which gifts are greater, and why. But what exactly is this gift of prophecy that is supposed to be so beneficial to the church, and is it still around today? Some people think it was one of the foundational gifts to the New Testament church (along with apostleship—see Ephesians 2:20), which died out with that first generation of Christians. Others think that prophecy is pretty much the same as preaching. Still others see it as a 'miraculous' type of gift, in which a person is given a direct revelation from God. The problem is that it is very difficult from the references we have in the New Testament to pin down exactly what this gift of prophecy is, and—perhaps more importantly—what it is not.

I think it helps to realize that prophecy in the New Testament does not simply take off where Old Testament prophets like Isaiah, Ezekiel, Amos, and others left off. Clearly the apostles like Peter, Paul, James and John have the central teaching role in the New Testament. So the New Testament prophets that Paul is talking about in 1 Corinthians 14 do not occupy the central role in passing on revelation from God. This was the role of the apostles, and what was revealed through them is available to everyone in the pages of the New Testament. Further, any prophecy in the New Testament was subject to the teaching of the apostles and therefore had less authority. That's exactly what we find in 1 Corinthians 14, where Paul says that any Corinthian prophecy should be weighed or tested (against Scripture) and in any case has less authority than Paul's words (v. 37).

In terms of the content of any prophet's message, it is clear that

Jesus and the gospel events are to take centre stage. The apostle John even tells us that testimony to Jesus is the spirit of prophecy (Revelation 19:10). So the task of the gospel age in which we live is preaching the gospel, both to ourselves and to outsiders. And Jesus remains God's final word to mankind (Heb 1:1-2). This means we should not expect to hear any Christian teaching that's additional to the Scriptures we already have. All that is yet to happen, in general terms, is the return of Jesus to judge the world and take his people to be with him (Heb 9:27-28). So because the Scriptures with their focus on Jesus take centre stage, the role and significance of prophets and prophecy is no longer central.

Nevertheless, if prophecy is something that is intelligible (that is, we can understand it), and if it builds up the church, then it is some sort of speaking gift, and could perhaps be a message about how the word of God applies to given situations in our lives. If it is one of the greater gifts, as Paul says it is, it should be both possible and desirable today.

So what can we say about this gift? We can say that although it is a gift, it is one that always needs to be weighed against the teaching of Scripture. We can say that although God through his Spirit gives it, it need not be miraculous or direct in nature. In fact, we probably already practise the gift of prophecy in our churches and meetings when Christian people share insights they have into the word of God and how it applies to our lives.

What we can say without doubt is that it should be practised in love (1 Corinthians 13) and with orderliness (1 Corinthians 14), for the benefit of the gathering of Christians.

The gift of healing

The gift of healing is also included in the list of gifts that Paul mentions in 1 Corinthians 12:8-10. But what is this gift and can we expect to see it today? Some churches appear to operate as though this is a central part of what the Spirit is doing in the world; others think that because Jesus did it, we ought to expect to be able to do it, or at least to see evidence of it in authentic gospel churches. Again, others think that this gift is no longer in operation. In thinking about these questions it helps to look at what the rest of Scripture says about this gift or ministry.

Healing in the Old Testament

There is some evidence of healing in the Old Testament—for example, Elijah healed a widow's only son in 1 Kings 17 and

Elisha healed a foreign dignitary called Naaman in 2 Kings 5. But examples are surprisingly few and far between and often have an evangelistic edge as the glory of God is revealed to people outside Israel. In the Old Testament, discussion of physical healing is closely connected (some would say entirely interwoven) with the spiritual healing of forgiveness and redemption. You can see the close connection in Psalm 103 and Isaiah 53.

Healing in the New Testament

There is evidence of healing in the New Testament, in the ministry of Jesus and the disciples. It often supports the preaching of the gospel, for example in Mark 1:29-39 and Acts 3, although there is not always a direct connection (see Acts 5:12-16). It is interesting to note that as the mission described in Acts progresses, there are fewer examples of the miraculous (healings, tongues, other miracles).

In the New Testament the verb for 'heal' is the same as the verb for 'save', so the close connection between physical and spiritual healing that we saw in the Old Testament continues in the New Testament. Jesus at times commands his disciples to heal the sick as they go out on mission trips (e.g. Matt 10:8; Luke 10:9), but he does not repeat this in the more general Great Commission that he leaves all his followers in Matthew 28:19-20.

In John 14:11-12 Jesus promises his disciples that they will do greater things than even he did, which many assume to be great miracles like healing. But the word translated in many of our Bibles as "miracles" in verse 11 is the Greek word for 'works' rather than the normal Greek word for 'miracles'. So it is likely that Jesus is referring to all his works, which in John's Gospel refers particularly to his work of revealing God to people. This could include miracles but definitely includes other things that reveal the Father to the world like preaching and teaching. Which means that the "greater things" Jesus says the disciples will perform in verse 12 more likely means a greater revealing of the Father, after the resurrection of Jesus, as the disciples spread the news of Jesus to the ends of the earth (as we saw in chapter 3).

Jesus' life and words also remind us that healings can sometimes work against belief. Just after he fed the 5000 in John 6, the crowd asked him for a miraculous sign to prove that he was "bread from heaven". What did they think they had just witnessed? And in Luke 16:19-31 in the parable of the rich man and Lazarus, Jesus basically says that if people don't believe the Scriptures, they won't believe even if someone is raised from the dead before their very eyes. This should give us some caution in expecting miracles to be great evangelistic devices.

The New Testament plainly expects healing to be a part of the life of the church. It is a gift to be practised in love by those who have that gift (1 Corinthians 12). But it is worth bearing in mind that the gift doesn't need to be limited to miraculous healings (miracle-working is listed separately in 1 Corinthians 12). And in James 5 the context suggests a strong connection to sin and forgiveness, so James may have had spiritual rather than physical healing at the front of his mind.

A place for healing today?

Putting all this together I think the Bible lets us say with confidence that God can and does heal, via the miraculous and the ordinary. But paired with this is the plain truth that healing is not the focus of God's work in the Old Testament, or of Jesus' ministry in the Gospels, or of the apostles' ministry in Acts, or of the church's ministry in the rest of the New Testament. So although it remains one aspect of the Christian life for us, it ought not to be the focus of our thoughts and energy.

Of course, there is plenty of encouragement to pray for healing and expect that God will work to heal people. So we should encourage people to pray for healing. But this is countered with the realization that God in his wisdom will heal some people and not others. It depends not so much on our faith (although our faith must be present) but on the purpose of God, who chooses to glorify himself sometimes in healing and other times in the faithful perseverance of his people, even unto death. God will always work for the good of his people, making us more like Jesus—whether that is in healing or in suffering.

As we think about this issue it is important to realize that people are not always able to balance all this stuff in their minds—hence our right desire to be wise and cautious in how we discuss the gift and the expectation of healing. At a practical level we need to be sensitive to people's reasonable suspicion about healings performed in God's name. We don't typically see the same sorts of healings today that we read about in the Bible—leprosy being healed immediately, withered hands being healed on the spot, people long dead being raised to life—so it's ok for people to reserve their judgement. If we saw healings like we read about in Scripture, people would be less suspicious, so caution is a reasonable position. There have been gross abuses of healing ministry in the past that continue to this day, sometimes with promises being made by ministers and Christians that should never have been made. These have had the effect of damaging people, and sometimes were intended only to make money off the gullible, which not only grieves us but which makes us understandably suspicious of miraculous claims.

So hopefully this quick look at what the Scriptures say and don't say on the topic of gifts has cleared things up a little for you. My genuine hope is that misunderstandings on this particular part of the work of the Holy Spirit don't distract us from all the great things we have already seen that he does for us and in us.

Feedback on this resource

If you enjoyed this Little Black Book, you might like to use the Facebook page as an easy way to let your friends know about it (as well as the other books in the series). And feel free to use the Facebook page to give me your feedback, comments and suggestions for future topics.

www.facebook.com/littleblackbooks

matthiasmedia

Matthias Media is an evangelical publishing ministry that seeks to persuade all Christians of the truth of God's purposes in Jesus Christ as revealed in the Bible, and equip them with high-quality resources, so that by the work of the Holy Spirit they will:

- abandon their lives to the honour and service of Christ in daily holiness and decision-making
- pray constantly in Christ's name for the fruitfulness and growth of his gospel
- speak the Bible's life-changing word whenever and however they can—in the home, in the world and in the fellowship of his people.

To find out more about our large range of very useful resources, and to access samples and free downloads, visit our website:

www.matthiasmedia.com

How to buy our resources

1. Direct from us over the internet:
   – in the US: www.matthiasmedia.com
   – in Australia and the rest of the world:
     www.matthiasmedia.com.au

2. Direct from us by phone:
   – in the US: 1 866 407 4530
   – in Australia: 1800 814 360 (Sydney: 9663 1478)
   – international: +61-2-9663-1478

3. Through a range of outlets in various parts of the world. Visit **www.matthiasmedia.com/contact** for details about recommended retailers in your part of the world, including www.thegoodbook.co.uk in the United Kingdom.

4. Trade enquiries can be addressed to:
   – in the US and Canada: sales@matthiasmedia.com
   – in Australia and the rest of the world: sales@matthiasmedia.com.au

> Register at our website for our **free** regular email update to receive information about the latest new resources, **exclusive special offers**, and free articles to help you grow in your Christian life and ministry.